PETS

Dogs

CHELSEA CLUBHOUSE

An Imprint of Chelsea House Publishers
A Haights Cross Communications Company

Philadelphia

June Loves

This edition first published in 2004 in the United States of America by Chelsea Clubhouse, a division of Chelsea House Publishers and a subsidiary of Haights Cross Communications.

Chelsea Clubhouse
1974 Sproul Road, Suite 400
Broomall, PA 19008-0914

The Chelsea House world wide web address is www.chelseahouse.com

Library of Congress Cataloging-in-Publication Data

Loves, June.
   Dogs / June Loves.
   v. cm. — (Pets)

   Contents: Dogs — Kinds of dogs — Parts of a dog — Puppies — Choosing pet dogs — Caring for pet dogs — Feeding — Exercising — Grooming — Bathing — Training — Visiting the vet — Dog shows — Wild dogs.

   ISBN 0-7910-7549-4
   1. Dogs—Juvenile literature. [1. Dogs. 2. Pets.] I. Title. II. Series: Loves, June. Pets.
   SF426.5.L68 2004
   636.7—dc21

                                                                        2002155665

First published in 2003 by
MACMILLAN EDUCATION AUSTRALIA PTY LTD
627 Chapel Street, South Yarra, Australia, 3141

Associated companies and representatives throughout the world.

Copyright © June Loves 2003
Copyright in photographs © individual photographers as credited

Page layout by Domenic Lauricella
Photo research by Legend Images

Printed in China

Acknowledgements

The author and the publisher are grateful to the following for permission to reproduce copyright material:

Cover photograph: boy with Dalmatian, courtesy of Getty Images.

ANT Photo Library, pp. 4, 15, 24, 27; Shane Armstrong, p. 14; A. & S. Carey—OSF/Auscape, pp. 13 (top); Jean-Paul Ferrero/Auscape, pp. 5, 10, 30; Jean-Michel Labat/Auscape, pp. 21, 23; Yves Lanceau/Auscape, p. 12 (bottom); Getty Images, pp. 1, 6, 7, 12 (top), 13 (bottom), 19; MEA Photo, p. 17 (scrubbing brush, toys); Photography Ebiz, pp. 8–9, 20, 25, 28, 29; Dale Mann/Retrospect, pp. 16–17, 18, 22; Sarah Saunders, p. 26; Victoria Police, p. 11.

With special thanks to The Pines Pet Centre, The Ark.

While every care has been taken to trace and acknowledge copyright, the publisher tenders their apologies for any accidental infringement where copyright has proved untraceable. Where the attempt has been unsuccessful, the publisher welcomes information that would redress the situation.

Contents

Dogs

Dogs are excellent pets. A dog will be a loyal friend for its whole life. Mixed-**breed** dogs, or mutts, are popular family pets.

Dogs need care and attention every day.

St. Bernards are large dogs.

Small dogs are happy to live indoors.
They also need to exercise outdoors.
Large dogs need a big space to live
in and plenty of exercise.

Kinds of Dogs

There are many kinds of pet dogs. They can be different sizes, shapes, and colors. Breeds are divided into eight different groups. Here are some examples.

Sporting dogs
- cocker spaniel
- golden retriever
- labrador retriever

Toy dogs
- chihuahua
- Maltese terrier
- toy poodle

Working dogs
- Great Dane
- Siberian husky
- rottweiler

A dalmatian is white with black spots.

Pedigree or pure-bred dogs are bred to have particular features.

Pugs are short-haired dogs with wrinkled faces.

Parts of a Dog

A dog is a **mammal**. A dog's tongue helps to keep its body cool when it pants. Dogs with erect ears hear better than dogs with floppy ears.

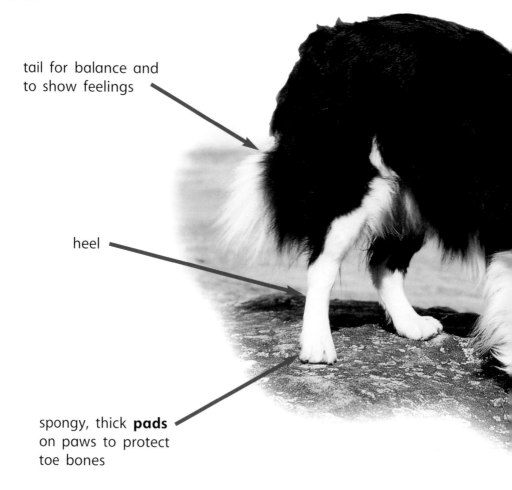

tail for balance and to show feelings

heel

spongy, thick **pads** on paws to protect toe bones

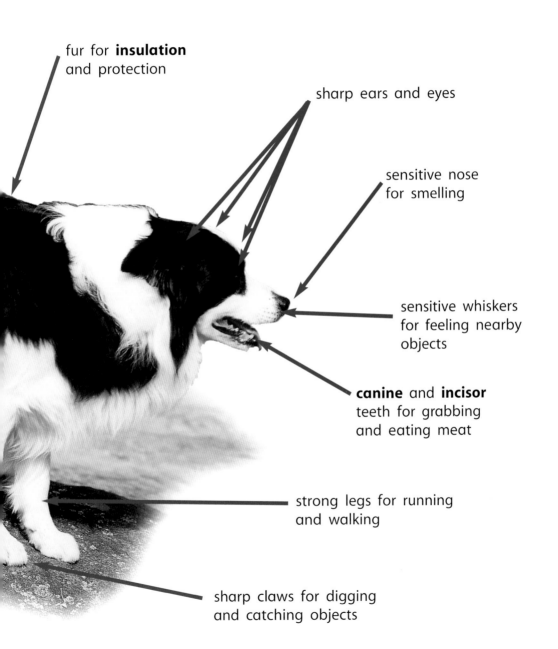

fur for **insulation**
and protection

sharp ears and eyes

sensitive nose
for smelling

sensitive whiskers
for feeling nearby
objects

canine and **incisor**
teeth for grabbing
and eating meat

strong legs for running
and walking

sharp claws for digging
and catching objects

9

Sense of smell

A dog uses its nose to sniff, **track**, and hunt for food. A dog also uses its sense of smell to check its surroundings and to get messages from other dogs.

A pointer makes this pose when it finds the animal it was tracking.

Some breeds of dogs have a keen sense of smell. They can be trained to find people, bombs, poisons, or drugs.

Rescue workers sometimes use search dogs with cameras on their heads.

Puppies

A female dog usually has between two and ten puppies in a **litter**. Puppies are born with their eyes and ears shut.

Puppies are helpless at birth.

Puppies drink milk from their mother for three to six weeks. They spend most of their time sleeping and eating.

Puppies are dogs that are younger than 12 months old.

After three weeks, most puppies start to explore the world around them. They start to play when they are about four weeks old.

When puppies are about five weeks old, they begin to run around. They are still wobbly on their legs.

Choosing Pet Dogs

Choose dogs that suit your family and home. Look for puppies or dogs that are healthy and friendly.

Some puppies grow into very big dogs that need lots of space, exercise, and grooming.

Animal shelters have many dogs and puppies that need homes.

A puppy can leave its mother when it is seven to nine weeks old. You can adopt homeless puppies or dogs from an animal shelter.

Caring for Pet Dogs

Prepare everything you need before you bring pet dogs home. These are some of the supplies you may want to care for your pet dog.

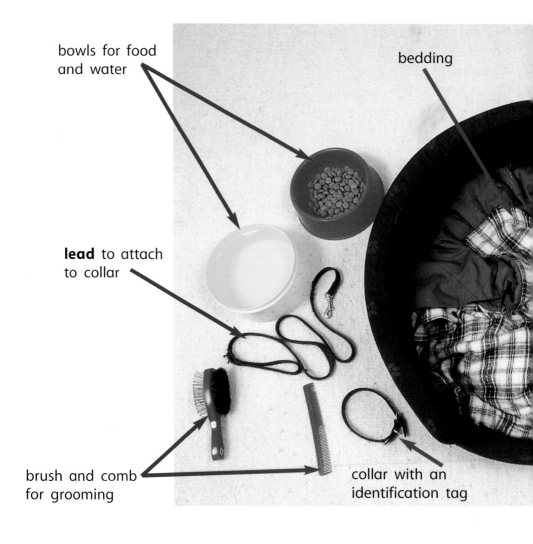

bowls for food and water

bedding

lead to attach to collar

brush and comb for grooming

collar with an identification tag

Wash your dog's bedding often to prevent **fleas** and other pests.

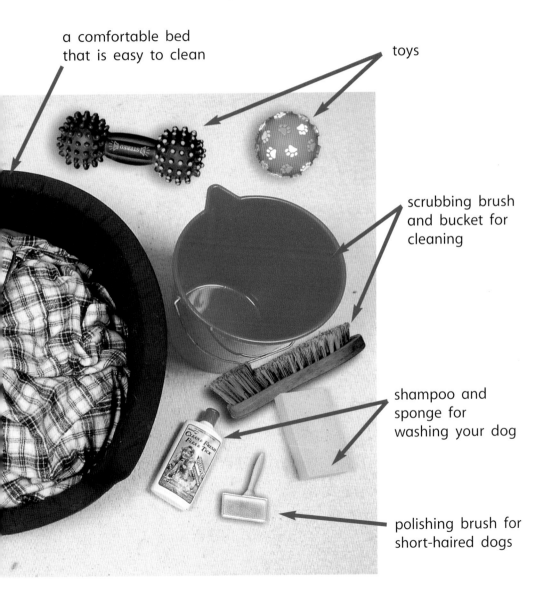

a comfortable bed that is easy to clean

toys

scrubbing brush and bucket for cleaning

shampoo and sponge for washing your dog

polishing brush for short-haired dogs

Feeding

Dogs need to be fed every day. Dogs can eat canned or dry food. A puppy should be fed puppy food for about nine months.

You can buy dog food from a pet store or supermarket.

Make sure your dog always has clean water.
Wash the food and water bowls every day.

Place your dog's food bowl in a quiet corner.

Exercising

All dogs need exercise to keep fit. You will need a collar and lead to take your dog for a walk.

Train your dog to walk by your side.

Most dogs love catching and throwing games. Some dogs also enjoy racing through an **agility** course. An agility course has tunnels and jumps. They are fun for dogs.

Dogs can jump over gates in an agility course.

Grooming

Most pet dogs need **grooming**. Grooming shows your dog that you care about it. Short-haired dogs need brushing every week to keep their fur and skin healthy. Long-haired dogs need grooming every day. Check for fleas at grooming time.

Afghan hounds are long-haired dogs that need grooming every day.

Bathing

Bathe your dog with warm water and dog shampoo. Then rinse its coat well and use a towel to dry it. Use a soft cloth or special brush to smooth or polish short-haired dogs' coats.

Baths keep dogs clean and smelling fresh.

Training

Training helps your dog to learn good behavior. You can train your dog to understand commands like "Sit!", "Stay!", "Come!", "Fetch!", and "Lie down!".

Reward your dog with praise and food treats when you train it.

Training dogs takes patience.

Be patient when you train your dog. Teach your dog one thing at a time. Keep lessons short and simple. Owners can learn how to train their dogs at dog obedience school.

Training dogs to work

Many dogs are trained to help their owners.
Hearing dogs are trained to alert owners
who are deaf to sounds, such as alarm
clocks, door bells, or smoke alarms.

Guide dogs are trained to
help people who are blind.

Assistance dogs are trained to help people who are **disabled** with everyday tasks, such as opening doors. They can operate buttons for elevators and traffic crossings. Herding dogs are trained to round up and drive sheep and cattle on farms.

Herding dogs are trained to work with animals such as cattle.

Visiting the Vet

When you get a puppy, take it to the **vet** for a check-up and **vaccinations**. Even if your dog seems healthy, it needs to visit the vet once a year. Your vet may talk to you about **neutering**.

Even adult dogs should visit the vet once a year.

Dog Shows

Dog shows are places where owners enter their pet dogs in competitions. Owners teach their dogs how to behave in the judging ring. The animals are judged and given points. The winners are awarded prizes.

Judges look for dogs with the best features.

Wild Dogs

Some wild dogs, such as dingoes, African hunting dogs, and wolves, live in packs. In the past, some people hunted wild dogs and moved into their **habitat**. Today many wild dogs are **endangered**.

Dingoes are wild dogs that live in Australia.

Glossary

agility	being able to move quickly and easily
breed	animals that belong to the same scientific group and have a similar appearance
canine	a long, sharp tooth near the front of the mouth
disabled	unable to use your body easily; people who are disabled may have trouble walking or using their arms
endangered	in danger of becoming extinct, or dying out
fleas	tiny insects that live in the fur of some animals; flea bites cause an animal's skin to itch
grooming	brushing or combing a pet to keep it clean
habitat	the place where animals or plants live
incisor	a short front tooth
insulation	a way of keeping heat and cold in or out
lead	a long rope that hooks to an animal's collar; also called a leash
litter	animals born at the same time to the same mother
mammal	a warm-blooded animal covered with hair whose young feed on their mother's milk
neutering	an operation that prevents an animal from having young
pads	leathery skin on the soles of the paws
pedigree	a pure-bred dog whose birth has been registered with an official dog club
track	to search by following the object's scent, or smell
vaccinations	medicine injected into people or animals to protect them from diseases
vet	a doctor who treats animals; short for veterinarian

Index